The Future in Law and Finance

The Future in Law and Finance

Inaugural Lecture
for the Chair in Law and Finance at
Erasmus School of Law, Erasmus University Rotterdam,
delivered on 26 April 2013

by

prof. dr. Alessio M. Pacces

eleven
international publishing

The author wishes to thank Ann van Beemen for editorial support and Sarah van den Brand for research assistance. Financial support by the Erasmus University of Rotterdam and the Erasmus School of Law is gratefully acknowledged.

Published, sold and distributed by Eleven International Publishing
P.O. Box 85576
2508 CG The Hague
The Netherlands
Tel.: +31 70 33 070 33
Fax: +31 70 33 070 30
e-mail: sales@budh.nl
www.elevenpub.com

Sold and distributed in USA and Canada
International Specialized Book Services
920 NE 58th Avenue, Suite 300
Portland, OR 97213-3786, USA
Tel: 1-800-944-6190 (toll-free)
Fax: +1-503-280-8832
orders@isbs.com
www.isbs.com

Eleven International Publishing is an imprint of Boom uitgevers Den Haag.

ISBN 978-94-6236-091-4
ISBN 978-94-6094-8589 (E-book)

Printed in The Netherlands

Table of contents

Rector Magnificus, esteemed colleagues, dear friends and family,

It is a great honour for me to stand before you today for this inaugural lecture as Professor of Law and Finance. I am grateful to the Executive Board of the Erasmus University and to the Board of Erasmus School of Law for their confidence. I will try to make the most of this wonderful opportunity given to me.

1. Introduction

This lecture will concern the role of the future in law and finance.[1]

To start with, I would say, finance is all about the future. By this I mean that financiers provide funds for investments, which will pay off in the future. Future output allows repayment of the funds borrowed to invest. The success of a capitalist economy depends on the ability of finance to sustain potentially infinite growth, funding today the output of tomorrow.[2]

If we could predict the future, finance would be trivial. However, because we actually do not know the future, finance is risky. Finally, because we act *as if* we could predict the future, finance can result in harm to society. The uncertainty of the future and the way we deal with this uncertainty make law important for finance.[3] Let me illustrate this with a few examples from the global financial crisis.

On the surface, the financial crisis that was sparked in 2007 is a story of poor investments, called subprime mortgages.[4] The important aspect, however, is that securitisation allowed creating safe assets from a pool of such risky investments.[5]

1 Law and finance, as I will explain below, is a branch of the economic analysis of law (law and economics) aiming to identify the legal rules that support economic growth by promoting efficient finance. See *infra* text to notes 26-31.

2 On the importance of finance for capitalism, see Levine (2005).

3 On the need to integrate macroeconomics and the problem of uncertainty in the economic analysis of law (law & economics), see Posner (2009) and Posner (2010) wherein a detailed, preliminary analysis of the global financial crisis is presented.

4 On the subprime mortgage crisis see Schiller (2008).

5 Gorton (2010b).

Figure 1 – Securitization of Subprime Mortgages

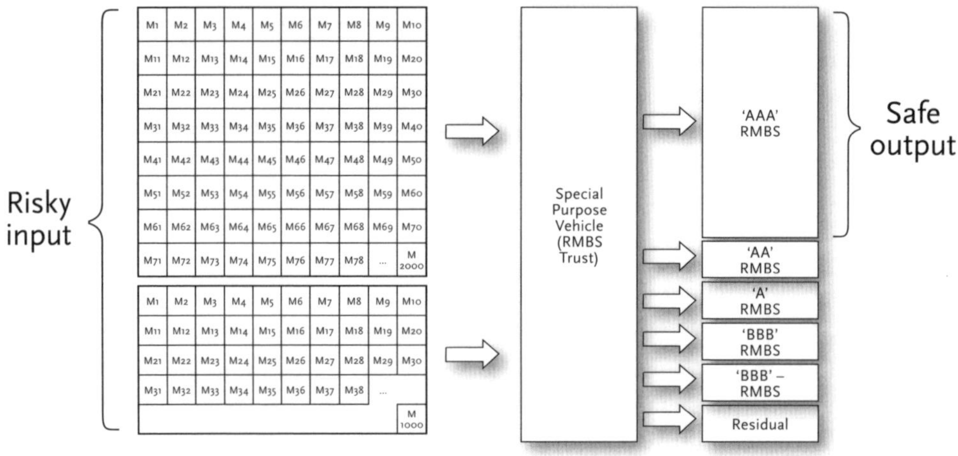

Source: Adapted from Gorton (2009).

Figure 1 shows, on the left side, securitisation pooling together thousands of subprime mortgages in an investment vehicle. More importantly, on the right side, the output of securitisation is different tranches of bonds with different ratings. The triple-A bonds have priority in repayment while the lower tranches are paid only if there is money available.

The losses are thus absorbed hierarchically, starting from the lowest tranche, up to the triple-B bonds and so forth. The triple-A bonds – about 80% of a typical deal – are expected to hardly ever experience any losses.

This example illustrates how finance can supposedly tame the future. If the future was, indeed, predictable, then finance could be safe. Securitisation allows a bank to finance risky investments offering the vast majority of lenders what they want, that is, safe assets to park their savings.[6] Here, law plays no role other than enforcing contracts between private parties.

Yet, since the future is not known, finance involves risk and some actors must bear it.[7] Risk is still assumed to be predictable. Predictability is good for incentives because those who voluntarily choose risk stand to lose or gain from it depending on their ability to accurately predict the future. This market discipline directs financial resources

6 On the global demand for safe assets stemming from financially underdeveloped emerging economies, see Caballero & Krishnamurthy (2011). On the consequences of this macroeconomic imbalance on global financial stability see Caballero & Farhi (2013). See also Roubini & Mihm (2010).

7 Tirole (2006: 199-235).

towards the best investment opportunities and ultimately promotes economic growth. The problem is that borrowers may renege on their promises to investors and hence escape market discipline. For want of a better word I call this 'cheating.' According to the law and finance scholarship,[8] the law should protect investors from cheating.

Figure 2 – Price of US Subprime-Related Securities

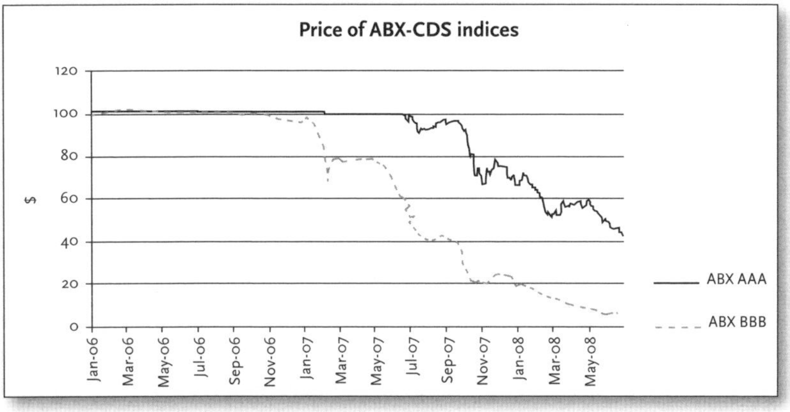

Source: International Monetary Fund (2008).

The story of subprime mortgages clearly shows that something went wrong with the market discipline.[9] In Figure 2 you can see the price of triple-B subprime bonds (the dotted line) dropping along with the U.S. housing market downturn since late 2006. This is good market discipline because those who financed the riskier slices of the subprime business faced losses when the risk materialized. But, in summer 2007, the price of triple-A bonds (the solid line) also started to fall. This was not supposed to happen.[10] Was it cheating?

Many believe that it was cheating,[11] but I beg to differ. Figure 2 shows that the price of triple-A subprime bonds had fallen by 60% in 2008 when they stopped trading. Yet, according to 2011 calculations, only 0.17% of these assets have experienced losses![12] In hindsight, tri-

8 The law and finance scholarship started with a homonymous article by La Porta, Lopez-de-Silanes, Shleifer, & Vishny (1998). I have discussed the achievements and the limitations of the law and finance scholarship in Pacces (2011).
9 See, in a similar vein, Hellwig (2009).
10 Caballero & Kurlat (2009).
11 Hellwig (2008); Calomiris (2009); Johnson & Kwak (2010).
12 Data analysis accounting for nearly 90% of subprime mortgages securitisations in the period 2004-2007 (Park 2011).

ple-A subprime securities were, indeed, quite safe. However, we had a financial crisis because their price was impaired.

There is another puzzle in this story. The losses from subprime mortgages could never be large enough to threaten the stability of the global financial system.[13] These losses turned out to be less than $70 billion, nearly all concentrated in the riskier tranches of securitisation.[14] This is a lot of money, but the size of the official U.S. banking system alone is about 200 times larger.[15] Subprime securities were more problematic for the safety they promised. Questioning the safety of about one trillion dollars of triple-A subprime securities got the banks in trouble.

Finance is prone to crises, and thus it is potentially harmful for societies, because *banking* makes the future look predictable although it is, in reality, uncertain and unpredictable.[16] Banks borrow money to finance risky investments whilst promising the safety of their short-term liabilities. Safety implies liquidity. In other words, these liabilities can be withdrawn at any time. One way to guarantee liquidity is to borrow against collateral that, like money, will be worth tomorrow as much as is worth today. Before summer 2007, triple-A subprime bonds were considered such collateral.[17] Borrowing against safe assets allowed banks to expand credit. However, although liquidity makes finance cheaper and more accessible, it creates systemic vulnerability.

---

13 Hellwig (2009); Gorton (2010a).

14 Park (2011).

15 According to the Federal Reserve Economic Data (FRED) collected by the Federal Reserve Bank of St. Louis, the total assets of US commercial banks are around $ 14 trillion.

16 Gorton (2012).

17 Gorton & Metrick (2012).

Figure 3 – Funding Structure of Commercial Banks (in U.S. $ billions)

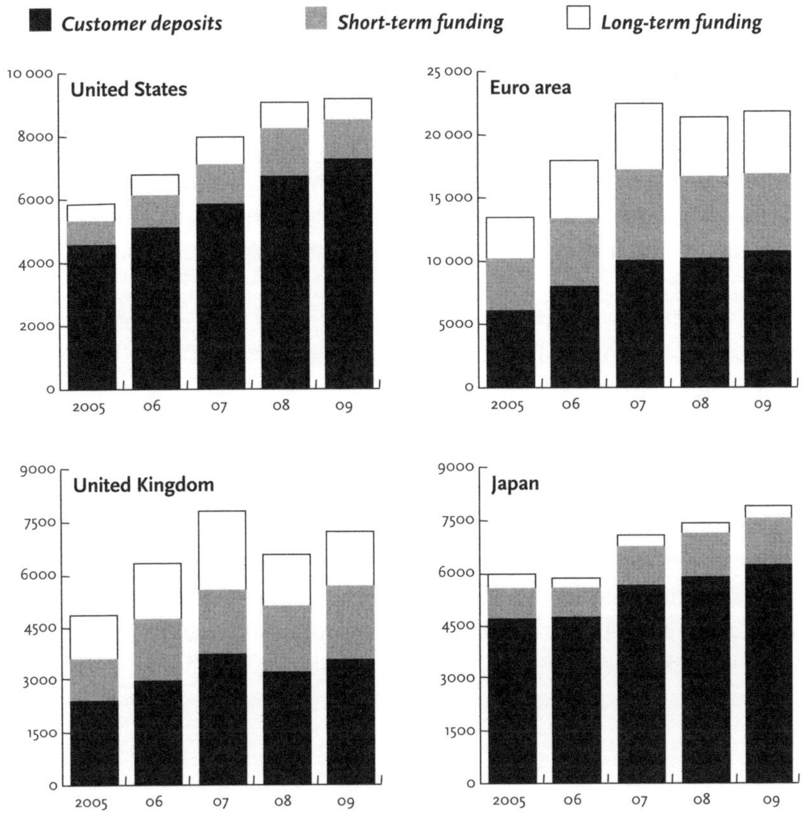

Source: International Monetary Fund (2010).

Figure 3 tells us why. The grey areas in the charts show the wholesale short-term liabilities only of commercial banks. In 2007, the wholesale short-term funding of banks in the U.S., the U.K. and the Eurozone exceeded $10 trillion.[18] If one trillion dollars of triple-A subprime bonds are no longer safe, investors suddenly seek to withdraw from about 10% of wholesale funding.[19] Such massive withdrawals force banks to sell assets at discount to make good on their promises of liquidity. At this point asset prices fall even though there is no fundamental reason for this to happen. Falling asset prices endanger the solvency of *any* bank, which depresses prices further. This downward spiral only stops when investors overcome the *uncertainty* about what the future price

18 This includes over $3 trillion short-term funding of US investments banks, not reported in Figure 3. See International Monetary Fund (2010).

19 The example oversimplifies the matter. In fact, wholesale investors cannot withdraw such large amounts at once. See *infra* text to notes 57-58.

of financial assets will be.[20] Until then, banks are so concerned about their solvency that they stop lending, and a recession ensues.

The subprime example shows that there can be no market discipline in the presence of uncertainty, because uncertainty compromises the prices upon which market discipline is based.[21] The global financial crisis occurred not because the banking system was insolvent, but because illiquidity was driving it to insolvency. Although markets eventually get things right, society may suffer from irreparable harm in the meantime.[22] In such a situation, law can intervene.

What can law do? In order to promote finance and economic growth, law should suspend market judgment in a crisis until the conditions for market discipline are restored.

I will argue for this assertion in the following manner. Firstly, I will explain what uncertainty is and why law and finance should pay attention to it. Secondly, I will discuss banking and the economic reasons for its regulation. Thirdly, I will argue that financial crises can only be stopped ex-post, and that conferring discretionary powers upon central banks is the only way to do this credibly. Fourthly, I will contend that the discretion of both central banks and private banks should be limited by appropriate governance rules. I will then conclude my lecture.

---

20 On the consequences of uncertainty on illiquidity and financial crises see Pacces (2013). See also Gorton & Ordoñez (2012) – for a model of collateral crises – and Caballero & Farhi (2013) – on the implications of shortage of safe assets for financial instability and economic policy.

21 See, in a similar vein, Dewatripont & Tirole (2012).

22 Zingales (2010).

2. Law & Finance under Uncertainty

What is uncertainty in economics and why is it important for the law? Lawyers often make fun of economists. Ronald Coase famously argued that how the law protects entitlements *does not matter* for efficiency in a world that does not exist, where contracting is costless.[23] He received a Nobel Prize in Economics,[24] not an Oscar in science fiction. Albeit counterintuitive, the Coase Theorem lays the foundations of law and economics, which aims to identify the legal rules maximizing social welfare in the real world.[25]

On the other hand, Andrei Shleifer became the most-cited living economist in the world showing, with his co-authors, that *law matters* for finance because it protects investors from cheating.[26] Lawyers might find that obvious but, ironically, Shleifer may miss his Nobel Prize only because of a financial scandal.[27] In fact, the finding that law matters for economic performance lays the foundation of law and finance. Law and finance aims to identify the legal rules promoting the growth of social welfare.[28]

The law and finance approach overlooks one important aspect of contracting. To sustain growth, individuals must contract about the future knowing very little about it. In the tradition of Frank Knight,[29] I call this lack of knowledge 'uncertainty'. Uncertainty differs from risk because it concerns events that cannot be assigned a probability, in other words, events that cannot be predicted. Cheating under asymmetric information is then only one reason why available finance may be less than optimal. A more fundamental reason is that, in the presence of uncertainty, parties may fail to agree on how to represent the future.

---

23 Coase (1960).

24 In his Nobel Prize lecture, Coase (1992) puts the famous Coase Theorem – that Coase never stated, at least in writing – in perspective.

25 Cooter & Ulen (2011).

26 La Porta, Lopez-de-Silanes, & Shleifer (2008) provide a broad overview of a decade of work by Shleifer and his co-authors on law and finance and the economic consequences of legal origins.

27 See Klick (2013) where the recent work by Shleifer is critically reviewed.

28 On the relationship between law, finance and economic growth see Levine (1999). The study of the relationship between finance and growth is plagued by endogeneity concerns. But see Rajan & Zingales (1998) for an empirical strategy to overcome it.

29 Knight (1921) was the first to explicitly distinguish uncertainty – concerning future events that cannot be assigned a probability – from risk – concerning events that can be assigned a probability. However, it is worth noting that, in the same period, Keynes (1921) was working on the notion of uncertainty within the probability theory.

Hence, I would argue that law and finance must deal with uncertainty as well.[30]

Investors who know less than managers about the use of their money cut lending until they obtain sufficient protection.[31] The law of bankruptcy, companies, and securities can help here and lower the cost of this protection. However, investors who cannot agree with managers on the probability that they will get their money back do not lend at all. This is not to say that investor protection is not important; but only that some problems are bigger than others.

To illustrate how large the consequences of uncertainty can be, let me point to the statistics for GDP growth the year following the peak of the financial crisis. In 2009, the U.S. GDP dropped by more than 3% while that of the Eurozone fell by over 4%. This is an aggregate loss exceeding one trillion dollars, almost 15 times larger than the losses from subprime mortgages.

Figure 4 – Rates of GDP growth for the U.S. and the EuroZone

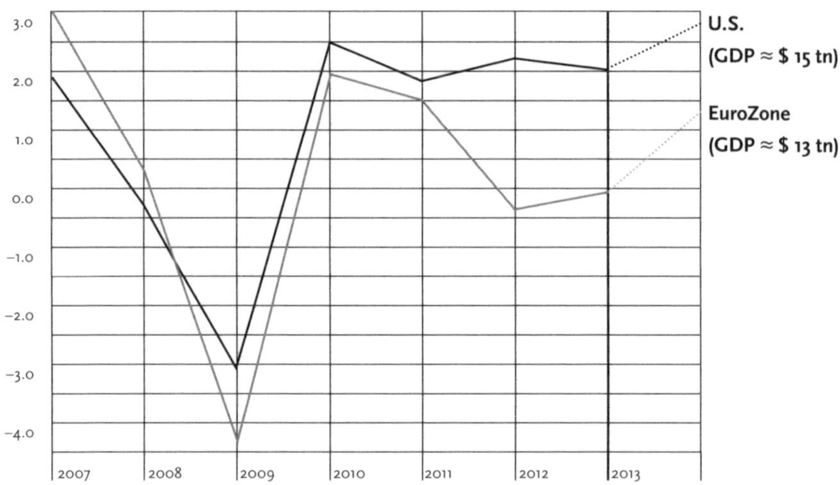

Source: Organization for Economic Co-operation and Development (2012).

Why is uncertainty revealed only in critical circumstances? Because people do not like uncertainty. This is confirmed by the resources we spend to overcome uncertainty. Consider the time we spend on setting our routines. We plan and conduct our lives as if the future was predict-

30 Within the law and economics scholarship, Pistor (2012) also contends that law and finance should be concerned with uncertainty and the financial instability stemming from it.
31 Tirole (2006: 237-282).

able; as do companies, governments and societies. In normal times, uncertainty is not visible and the future is handled as routine. Financial exchange does occur based on a probabilistic approach to risk and different preferences towards it.

John Maynard Keynes was the first to argue that this way to deal with the future is *conventional*.[32] In order to justify our decisions despite uncertainty, we must rely on probabilities. Probabilistic models of risk assessment are based on a convention that the future will be like the past. Such convention is not set in stone. It lasts for as long as it is validated by the future. When circumstances appear to deny the validity of the convention, for instance, when something happens that was not included in modelling the future, uncertainty is back to the forefront. When uncertainty reigns, financial markets freeze until a new convention to handle the future is established. Firms deprived of credit invest less, lay off employees, and eventually go bankrupt. According to Keynes, the instability of capitalism depends on the fragility of our conventions to handle the future.

To cope with financial instability, legal institutions should support these conventions when they are disrupted. For many, Keynes was a precursor of behavioural economics;[33] but it is not irrational to resolve uncertainty relying on conventions. Conventional risk assessment allows us to deal with the future consistently and to the best of our knowledge. Professionals of the financial industry do this for a living. It is tempting for the law to challenge probabilistic risk assessment when it fails to predict the future. Such paternalism, however, is unwarranted if individuals behave rationally.[34] On the other hand, the presence of uncertainty also counsels against regulatory reliance on market discipline when prices are impaired.[35] Financial crises are like Hegel's night, where all cows are black.[36] As it is impossible to distinguish cheating from market malfunctioning, punitive measures against cheating must wait for market discipline to be restored.

What should the law do then? It should make sure that governments respond to a financial crisis in the right way.[37] The challenge is to end uncertainty before it is too late without incentivising behaviours condu-

32 Keynes (1936: Chapter 12). On the Keynes' approach to uncertainty, see recently Roncaglia (2012).

33 See e.g. Akerlof & Shiller (2009).

34 This point applies as well to softer form of paternalism, e.g. the so-called 'libertarian paternalism' (Thaler & Sunstein, 2003).

35 Frydman & Goldberg (2011).

36 Hegel (1807).

37 See, in a similar vein, Levine (2011).

cive to the next crisis. Because we are unable to predict the future, the promise to prevent financial crises is unrealistic. However, a credible and transparent backstop, established by law, can deal with a crisis *after* it has occurred. Setting this backstop *ex-ante* can also avoid compromising private incentives, if the backstop is designed to fall back on market discipline when the dust settles. Only a credible commitment to stop disaster can validate the promise to restore market discipline.

3. Banking and Financial Crisis

Uncertainty is not enough to cause a financial crisis. If that was the case we would face a crisis whenever a flight or one of our PhD students was late; by the way, that happens too often to be critical. Uncertainty is a problem when it concerns significant issues. However, 9/11 and the stock market crash of 2000 created a lot of uncertainty, but they did not trigger any financial crisis. Why? Because a financial crisis is always about *debt*.[38] This leads us to the issue of the vulnerability of the system: the banks.

Hyman Minsky, a Keynesian economist of the last century, appropriately defined banks 'merchants of debt.'[39] The highly-stylized balance sheet in figure 5 illustrates *how* banks trade debt. Banks lend on the long-term basis and borrow on the short-term basis, typically in the form of deposits, but also in the wholesale market. (They borrow on the long-term basis as well, but I am not dealing with this aspect here). Banks profit from maturity transformation, namely, from the interest spread between long-term assets and short-term liabilities.[40] To put it simply, take this spread for granted and equal to, say, 4% minus 2%. Given the spread, the higher the debts and the bank's leverage, the larger are the profits from maturity transformation.

Figure 5 – A Bank's Stylized Balance Sheet

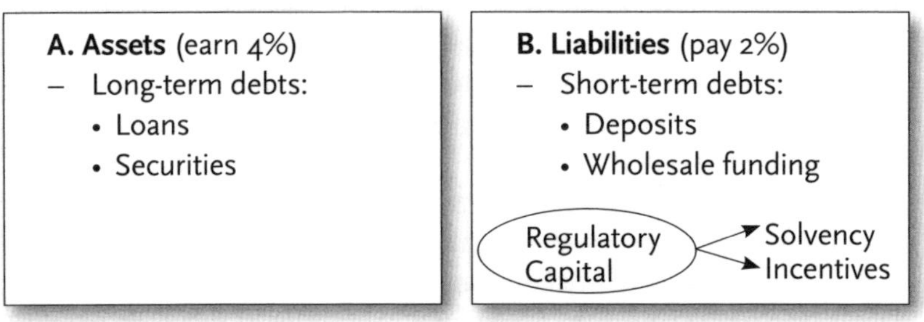

The danger of maturity transformation is that the bank's short-term liabilities carry the promise of *liquidity*. The money at your bank is safe because you can withdraw it at any time. Whether you do this via cash, cards, or cheques is unimportant: the banks' liability *is* money

38 Gorton (2012).
39 Minsky (1986: 279).
40 Pacces (2010).

even if you don't physically see it. But remember, your money is not in the bank's vault; it is invested somewhere in the world where it yields more than it costs the bank to borrow it from you. The bank is promising you liquidity against illiquid assets. Isn't this misleading?

Yes and no. Individually, you can effectively withdraw your money because the bank will have enough cash to pay you back. But unless you spend all your savings, you will have to do something with that cash, namely look for another safe asset to park it. You'll soon find out that all safe assets are based on the same misconception regarding liquidity. The misconception, in fact, is not an individual, but systemic. The bank is unable to make good on the promise of liquidity if *all* depositors withdraw simultaneously. But, think carefully, there is only one situation when this is likely to happen: when depositors fear that the bank's assets aren't worth enough to pay them back. Whether this is true or not is irrelevant because people's perception becomes their reality. The fear of insolvency determines illiquidity which, in turn, results in insolvency. Thus, it becomes a self-fulfilling prophecy. It is called *bank run.*[41]

Running at a bank is anti-social, because for any non-negligible size of the bank in question, the problem is likely to spread to the whole banking system. The other banks usually don't have a clear picture of how much the assets of the troubled bank are worth. They would need time to decide whether to support, at a profit, the bank concerned. But there is no time available in a bank run: illiquidity kills quickly.[42] In addition, because banks manage scarce amounts of cash efficiently, banks are variously exposed to one another: therefore, illiquidity will kill them quickly too. A bank run, however unfounded, can cripple an entire banking system.

You may still feel no sympathy for banks because you do not see how their misleading methods can possibly benefit society. Here the importance of uncertainty becomes apparent. Banks help overcome it, by dealing with the future based on a conventional risk assessment.[43] But they offer their short-term creditors, including depositors, a simple promise of liquidity. In so doing, they bear every uncertainty not included in the conventional risk models.

41 Diamond & Dybvig (1983).

42 Mehrling (2011) illustrates the severity of liquidity problems in a broader perspective than the traditional bank runs.

43 Drawing on Keynes' *General Theory* (1936), Minsky (1975) elaborated and expanded on the role of banking in overcoming uncertainty in finance.

Liquidity is important for a capitalist economy because investments are long-term but we, as individuals, are generally unwilling to commit our savings for many years to come. This reluctance, to be sure, is not dependent on our inability to calculate conventional probabilities (you could always hire a professor of finance for that), but rather on the distrust we have that these probabilities effectively represent the future. Our demand for liquidity – as Keynes put it – is the measure of this distrust.[44] Satisfying this demand, banks can finance an important portion of real investments. But to keep banks going, never question the safety they promise.

Banking regulation is there to remedy banks' fragility. Thanks to regulation, bank runs have become almost obsolete. The U.S. created deposit insurance with the Banking Act of 1933 and most countries of the developed world followed suit. In the E.U., deposit insurance is harmonized by the 1994 Directive on Deposit Guarantee Schemes, setting the minimum coverage at 100.000 Euros as of 2010.[45] Due to deposit insurance, small depositors do not need to worry about the quality of the bank's assets. The safety net of banks includes other tools:[46] the lender of last-resort facilities operated by the central bank and an implicit commitment by governments to bailing out key banks. The presence of this safety net inevitably leads to some moral hazard in banking.

To those who still regard moral hazard as arcane law and economics jargon, I recommend watching Wall Street 2.[47] Moral hazard is as simple as cheating. Because the state ultimately guarantees most of the banks' liabilities, creditors do not bother to discipline banks and shareholders have incentives to engage in excessive risks and leverage. If things go well, they'll gain; if things go wrong, taxpayers will foot the bill. Therefore, regulation requires banks to hold a certain amount of equity in exchange for the safety net.[48] Again look at the bank's stylized balance sheet in figure 5. Limiting leverage, regulatory capital serves two functions: it buffers against insolvency; and it incentivises shareholders and their managers to take less risk as they stand to lose more in case of failure. This is the mantra of the international standards

44 Keynes (1937: 216). See also Runde (1994).

45 Directive 94/19/EC of 30 May 1994 on deposit-guarantee schemes (OJ L 135, 31.5.1994) as amended by Directive 2009/14/EC of 11 March 2009 (OJ L 68, 13.3.2009).

46 Heremans & Pacces (2012: 579-581).

47 In the film 'Wall Street: Money Never Sleeps' (known as Wall Street 2, 2010), the character Gordon Gekko – played by Michael Douglas – put it as simply as possible: 'Moral hazard is when they take your money and then are not responsible for what they do with it.'

48 Heremans & Pacces (2012: 584-589).

informing the regulation of bank capital. These standards are known as various releases of the Basel Accords.[49]

On April 16 2013, the European Parliament agreed to implement Basel 3 with a Capital Requirements Regulation and a Capital Requirements Directive set to enter into force in 2014.[50] The Regulation will ensure the uniform application of Basel 3 throughout the European Union. Because Basel 3 aims at strengthening the capital requirements of banks, this sounds like good news against moral hazard. However, I will argue that moral hazard is not a key determinant of financial crises. To be clear, I am not implying that moral hazard does not matter – it does and I'll return to it later.[51] Once again, there are some problems that are bigger than others.

The global financial crisis was a crisis of so-called 'shadow banking.'[52] Banks were still profiting from financing long-term investments with short-term debt. However, they were doing it in a new way, using long-term assets as collateral to borrow from large investors. You do not even have to be a bank to do this. This is shadow banking precisely because it is out of the regulatory perimeter. As it is not subject to capital regulation, it has formally no access to the safety net.

Despite the absence of deposit insurance, shadow banking could guarantee the liquidity of liabilities as long as the collateral had a stable market price. The repo, a typical form of collateralized borrowing, illustrates this well. Look at figure 6. The repo is a loan made of two

49 The Basel Accords are international standards set by the Basel Committee on Banking Supervision created in 1974 under the auspices of the Bank of International Settlement established in Basel. There are three releases of the Basel Accords (short of their various amendments): Basel 1 (1988), Basel 2 (2004), and Basel 3 (2010). Basel 2 was supposed to be implemented in 2008 but, due to the financial crisis, it has been effectively superseded by Basel 3. The Basel Accords are not legally binding so long as they are not implemented by some legislative instruments at the national or supranational level.

50 The implementation of Basel 3 in the E.U. is based on the negotiations (known as 'Trialogue') between the European Parliament, the Commission and the Council under the ordinary legislative procedure (formerly co-decision, Art 289 TFEU). The outcome of these negotiations was published by the Council on 27 March 2013 and approved by the Parliament on 16 April 2013. After the final vote of the Council and the publication in the EU Official Journal, the two legislative instruments will come into force. See 'Bank capital rules: Council confirms agreement with European Parliament', press release (with a link to the text agreed upon) available at www.consilium.europa.eu/uedocs/cms_data/docs/pressdata/en/ecofin/136581.pdf (last accessed on 12 June 2013).

51 See *infra* text to notes 95-105.

52 Shadow banking is broadly defined as the set of 'entities and activities outside the regular banking system that perform bank-like functions' (Financial Stability Board 2011). For two different, but complementary perspectives on shadow banking, see Gennaioli, Shleifer & Vishny (2013) and Gorton & Metrick (2012).

transactions. In the opening transaction, the borrower deposits securities at the lender and receives the cash to purchase the securities; the cash received is equal to the price of the securities minus an X%, which is called 'haircut.'[53] In the closing transaction, the borrower pays back the money plus some interest and gets her securities back. Repos' maturity is very short, typically overnight. Repos are terminated when a previous position is not renewed. However legally constructed, repos are exempted from bankruptcy law.[54] In the U.S., the bankruptcy code was amended in 1984 and in 2005 to create a safe harbour for repos.[55] Likewise, in the E.U., the Directives on Settlement Finality and Financial Collateral Arrangements exempt repos from ordinary bankruptcy procedures.[56] As a result, if the borrower fails to deliver at termination of the contract, the lender can immediately sell the collateral. Because the haircut is the excess value of collateral relative to the loan, the haircut determines the safety of repo.

Figure 6 – Typical Funding of Shadow Banks (Repo)

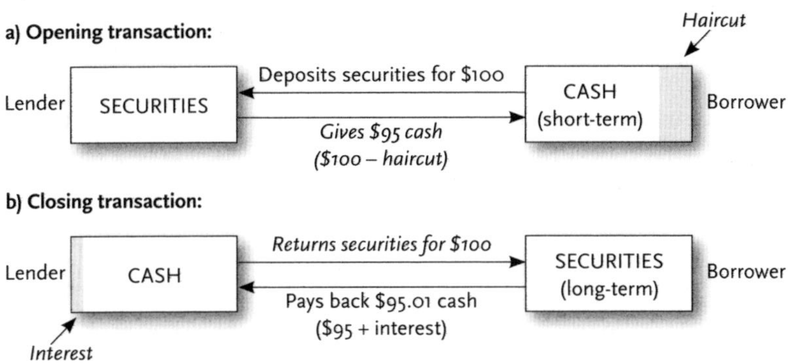

Remember how the financial crisis started.[57] About one trillion dollars of triple-A subprime securities lost their status of safe assets. Investors who doubt the quality of collateral can run similarly to depositors. However, large investors cannot run at once because the stock of safe assets in the world is limited. What investors can do is to recreate

53 Gorton & Metrick (2010a).
54 See Perotti (2010).
55 See 11 U.S.C. § 101(47) and § 559. See also Duffie & Skeel (2012).
56 Directive 98/26/EC of 19 May 1998 on settlement finality in payment and securities settlement systems (OJ L 166/45, 11.6.1998) and Directive 2002/47/EC of 6 June 2002 on financial collateral arrangements (OJ L 168/43, 27.6.2002) as subsequently amended.
57 See *supra* text to notes 15-22.

the safety of their loans by raising the haircuts.[58] In this way, investors gradually withdraw from repos and invest the surplus in the few safe assets left, for instance U.S. Treasury bonds.

But the consequences of raising haircuts can be disastrous. For example, imagine that triple-A subprime securities are financed with a haircut of 5%. You, a shadow bank, have $1 million invested in securities worth 20 million. Assume that speculations on housing market downturn make the price drop a little, say from 100 to 99. The securities are now worth $19 million and 800,000. You have lost $200,000. More importantly, you can refinance only $16 million and must sell $3.8 million of securities. Because less than $200,000 of capital that you have lost is needed to purchase them, this forced sale is unlikely to affect price.[59] So if the haircut doesn't change, the price doesn't drop; and perhaps it returns to 100 after a while.

On the other hand, the situation is different if lenders become nervous that price will drop further and raise the haircut.[60] Imagine, for simplicity, that the haircut goes up as high as 10%. You can now refinance $8 million, but must sell $11.8 million, which can be borrowed on the market if others put down $1.18 million. Even if other intermediaries have this capital at hand,[61] they are unlikely to commit it unless they can be sure that price will not drop below a certain floor. Increasing haircuts reflect precisely this lack of certainty.[62] Like a bank run, increasing haircuts determine a self-fulfilling prophecy that the price of certain assets will drop. This may lead to bankruptcy of all intermediaries that invested in those assets.

Falling into this trap is no evidence of moral hazard.[63] Shadow

---

58 For a formalized model on how this behaviour occurs under conditions of asymmetric information, see Dang, Holmström & Gorton (2012). For another explanation, based on uncertainty, see Krishnamurthy (2010). The two approaches are not mutually exclusive. Whether episodes of 'flight to quality' (Caballero & Krishnamurthy, 2008) depend on uncertainty, on asymmetric information, or on both is an open question that can be answered only empirically.

59 In the literature on asset pricing, forced sales that depress price are labelled 'fire sales.' See Shleifer & Vishny (2011). According to finance theory, it is very difficult to start fire sales. However, fire sales happen, particularly in a financial crisis.

60 Raising haircuts reduce funding liquidity, which impairs market liquidity, which in turn feeds back on funding liquidity via falling asset prices. See Brunnermeier & Pedersen (2009).

61 For the U.S., He, Khang & Krishnamurthy (2010) provide evidence that, in key moments of the global financial crisis, bank capital (specifically of commercial banks) was available in the aggregate.

62 See Geanakoplos (2010).

63 I have developed this argument in more detail in Pacces (2013).

banking did not enjoy government guarantee. Financial regulators and supervisors barely knew that shadow banking existed. Shadow banking was eventually bailed out along with the banks that sponsored it.[64] This happened because bailout is unavoidable when the safety net is not prepared for financial innovation. But this circumstance does not imply that the banks' creditors *could count* on bailout. If that was the case, there would have been no run. In fact, there was hardly any run on insured deposits. So the problem was not lack of market discipline.

The main problem with banking is externalities.[65] In the face of uncertainty, banks promise more safety than is socially optimal, overexposing the system to disruptive banking crises. In the analysis of Hyman Minsky,[66] banks always seek innovative ways to profitably increase the size of their balance sheet.[67] To keep up with increasing promises of liquidity, banks must incur more and more short-term debts. A crisis occurs when such debts cannot be refinanced. Minsky wrote before securitization. Securitization created opportunities for financing where there was none. But securitisation also allowed financing some poor businesses. Banks engaged in this innovation not because they could expect to be spared the losses, but because the anticipated losses were far lower than the costs of a financial crisis for society.

The bad news, again heralded by Minsky, is that the externalities of banking cannot be prevented.[68] It is too easy to engage in innovative forms of banking and get around regulation through unregulated entities or activities. Shadow banks demonstrate that anybody can engage in banking if only they can guarantee the conventional safety of short-term liabilities. Yesterday, we know, the problem was repo; but what about tomorrow? Imagine that some complicated technology to promise safety against long-term investments is invented 20 years from now. Call it 'rocket-science bond.' Before regulators realize the externalities of the new technology, the harm will already have been done.

---

64 Gorton (2010b) and Brunnermeier (2009).

65 Brunnermeier, Crockett, Goodhart, Persuad, & Shin (2009).

66 Minsky (1986).

67 On the relationship between liquidity and leverage see Adrian & Shin (2010).

68 Minsky (1986: 279-282).

4. Regulatory Discretion in an Uncertain World

Having talked about how banking contributes to financial instability, I will now go on to discuss bank regulation and, in particular, why it must rely on the discretion of central banks to deal with financial crises effectively.

If there is uncertainty, banks are not driven by moral hazard. Hence, higher capital requirements cannot stop banks from taking excessive risk. However, capital adequacy can make banks safer by forcing them to operate on a lower scale. The uniform implementation of Basel 3 in the E.U. is consistent with this goal. The Capital Requirements Regulation will increase bank capital moderately, eventually capping risk-weighted leverage at around 22 times the equity.[69] Commentators have advocated stricter limits to improve solvency.[70] This would be like tripling the check-in time for flying. I leave it for you to decide whether the near certainty that you will never miss a flight is worth this wait.[71]

More importantly, Basel 3 allows bank supervisors to set additional capital buffers. In the E.U., these provisions are included in the Capital Requirements Directive,[72] approved by the European Parliament along with the Capital Requirement Regulation.[73] The Directive allows the competent supervisors to impose contingent payout restrictions until the capital of banks is increased to levels well above the minimum requirements. This measure aims to improve solvency with the right timing. It prevents the banks' balance sheet from growing too much in good times, while allowing leverage to accommodate losses in bad times.[74] Moreover, payout restrictions may counter the short-termism

---

69 Art. 87 of the forthcoming Capital Requirement Regulation (henceforth CRR proposal) compels banks to maintain at least 4.5% of their risk-weighted assets in the form of Tier 1 common equity (within a 8% of total capital requirement). See Council of the E.U., 'Proposal for a Regulation of the European Parliament and of the Council on prudential requirements for credit institutions and investment firms (Text of the political agreement, 26 March 2013).

70 See, authoritatively, Admati & Hellwig (2013).

71 On the trade-offs of capital requirements see Dewatripont, Rochet & Tirole (2010: 52-55).

72 Art. 123 and 124 of the forthcoming Capital Requirement Directive (henceforth CRD proposal). See Council of the E.U., Proposal for a Directive of the European Parliament and of the Council on the access to the activity of credit institutions and the prudential supervision of credit institutions and investment firms and amending Directive 2002/87/EC of the European Parliament and of the Council on the supplementary supervision of credit institutions, insurance undertakings and investment firms in a financial conglomerate (Text of the political agreement, 26 March 2013).

73 See *supra* note 50.

74 Countercyclical payout restrictions were long advocated, among others, by Minsky (1986: 356-7).

of bank shareholders along with other corporate governance rules, which I'll discuss later.

Yet, if you believe the externality story, you do not want to focus on capital. Financial crises wipe out capital quickly. The priority is, rather, to fix *liquidity*.

The Capital Requirement Regulation does a poor job of this. Passively implementing the Liquidity Coverage Ratio and Net Stable Funding Ratio of Basel 3,[75] the Regulation will eventually impose a short-term and a long-term constraint on the liquidity that banks can promise against their illiquid assets. The problem with this approach is threefold: first, nobody knows the optimal ratio of maturity transformation by banks; second, even if we knew what is optimal today, innovation might change this tomorrow; and third, such an inflexible approach is an open invitation to get around liquidity regulations through institutions not subject to it.

Other proposals to regulate liquidity *ex-ante* have similar shortcomings. For instance, authoritative commentators on both sides of the Atlantic suggested making the bankruptcy law exceptions for repos conditional on the payment of a fee for insuring the collateral.[76] This is reminiscent of deposit insurance. But, even overlooking that the horses of repo have bolted, deposit insurance has never been a real insurance scheme.[77] Particularly in systemic events, it is actually a government guarantee, which makes it effective. Due to the unique authority to tax future generations, only governments can insure systemic risk without having to post collateral themselves.[78] Although it is a good idea to insure liquidity when it is widely promised on the market, it is an illusion

75 See Art. 401 and 401a of the CRR proposal. The Liquidity Coverage Ratio (LCR) is a regulatory tool that will require banks to hold an amount of liquid assets sufficient to withstand a 30-day shock in short-term funding. The Net Stable Funding Ratio (NSFR) is a longer-term instrument that will determine the proportion of stable liabilities (deposits and long-term debt) necessary to fund illiquid assets. Both the LCR and the NSFR will require implementing measures by the European Banking Authority (EBA) and will be phased in only gradually (see Art. 444, 481 and 481a of the CRR proposal). On the liquidity regulation recommended by Basel 3, including the expected implementation timeline, see the documents of the Bank for International Settlements available at www.bis.org/bcbs/basel3.htm.

76 See, most prominently, Gorton & Metrick (2010b) and Perotti & Suarez (2009). Other commentators have expressed darker views on the exemption of repos and derivatives from the automatic stay in bankruptcy law. See Duffie & Skeel (2012) for a discussion.

77 Acharya & Öncü (2013: 330) make a similar point.

78 See Caballero & Kurlat (2009), discussing *inter alia* a realistic proposal on how to introduce an insurance scheme for systemic risk.

to aim to discipline banks by asking them a price they will never be able to pay.

Because central banks deal in financial assets to conduct monetary policy, they can support the liquidity of these assets better than governments can support the institutions investing in them.[79] Moreover, focusing on assets instead of institutions,[80] central banks can effectively discipline liquidity *ex-post*. Crucially, they will have to follow the old Bagheot's rule of lending of last resort, that is, lend freely, against good collateral, and with penalty.[81] Following this rule is sufficient to suspend market discipline when it is impaired; but it is also necessary to restore market discipline after the turmoil.[82]

Lending of last resort by central banks can stop a financial crisis for as long as necessary to distinguish illiquidity from insolvency. More importantly, it can stop illiquidity from resulting in massive insolvency. Hence, it can stop the externalities of banking.

This backstop does not compromise incentives as long as it is *temporary*.[83] In a crisis, central banks, rather than private markets, should identify distressed assets and accept them as collateral. But they should set conservative haircuts to avoid making losses, and charge enough for liquidity to disallow profit by borrowing institutions. In this way the capital of borrowing institutions is frozen, but so is the downward spiral of asset prices. Having set a ceiling for haircuts, the central bank will effectively lend only to the institutions on the verge of insolvency. Those that do not have enough capital to maintain the haircuts will have to be resolved.[84] Resolution of insolvency is essential to get out of a crisis effectively. Central banks are supposed to suspend market discipline when it is impaired, not to sustain zombie banks indefinitely.

---

79 Mehrling (2011) notably advocates a role as dealer of last resort (as an evolution of the traditional role of lender of last resort) for the U.S. Central Bank.

80 Acharya & Öncü (2013) also recommend focusing on assets instead of institutions. However, they suggest the institution of a (Repo) Resolution Authority to support the liquidity of distressed assets, with central banks operating exclusively as lender of last resort towards the Resolution Authority.

81 Bagehot (1873).

82 Other commentators have recommended suspending market discipline when prices are impaired during a financial crisis. See, most notably, Frydman & Goldberg (2011). The problem with this approach is to define price impairment out of a certain range of values. However, if one accepts the idea that a range of 'right prices' cannot be predetermined, the only solution is to confer the discretion to suspend market discipline upon an authority with the right incentives. This is the solution being advocated in this lecture. See Acharya & Öncü (2013) for a similar approach.

83 See, in a broader perspective, De Grauwe (2012).

84 See Pacces (2013) for more elaboration on this proposal.

Legislatures are reluctant to openly empower central banks because, in the eyes of the public, emergency lending is often confused with bailout. A bailout, however, is a capital injection, which is implicit when you lend to a bankrupt institution. Excessive concerns for moral hazard typically delay intervention until bailout is the only way to avoid disaster.[85] But this distortion would be unwarranted if the central bank had *initially* a mandate to intervene in a liquidity crisis and to lend *exclusively* to solvent institutions. Central banks can efficiently stop uncertainty if they commit to lending, on these terms, against assets that are distressed in a crisis.

Contrary to the current regulatory trend, this approach calls for discretion on two sides: central banks and banking institutions. In a hypothetical world in which central banks decide which assets to support in order to stop a financial crisis, we still need to trust central bankers to do the right thing and private banks not to abuse the backstop. When uncertainty is resolved, moral hazard is indeed a problem calling for governance solutions.

85 Reinhart & Rogoff (2009) document that the direct cost of bailing out banks is negligible compared to the macroeconomic consequences of a banking crisis.

5. Governance and Accountability

I am now going to explain how central banks and private banks can be accountable, if they have the right governance.

Some believe that powerful central bankers, like Mr. Bernanke and Mr. Draghi, are saving the world.[86] As I am a cynical economist, I think they are simply responding to their incentives. Since regulation affects incentives, whether central bankers are good at their job also depends on the law.

Central bankers care mainly about their prestige, which is linked to the reputation of the institution they are heading. The major achievement of central banks in the past decades has been independence from their government. For central banks, worse than losing independence is the disruption of the financial system they are responsible for. This briefly explains the unorthodox policy interventions by central banks around the world since the beginning of the financial crisis.[87] Central bankers understood that problems of collateral were driving asset prices. They intervened massively, even beyond their lender of last resort powers, and bailed out financial institutions when there was no alternative. Particularly Bernanke had the courage to risk independence in order to avoid financial meltdown.[88]

Many believe that the Federal Reserve could not do this again because the Dodd-Frank Act, enacted in 2010 as a response to the financial crisis, now limits its discretionary powers.[89] Here again, I beg to differ because, as I explained, no amount of commitment to avoid bailout is credible if there is no alternative. However, the Dodd-Frank Act now provides such an alternative by establishing credible resolution mechanisms ultimately backed by the Treasury.[90] As long as this mechanism is effective, it will allow the Federal Reserve to focus on illiquidity – as it should be.

---

86 See Wyplosz (2012b).

87 For a recent overview of these issues by three world's leading monetary economists, see Reichlin, Turner, & Woodford (2013).

88 Bernanke (2012).

89 Dodd-Frank Wall Street Reform and Consumer Protection Act (Dodd-Frank Act), Pub. L. No. 111-203, 124 Stat. 1376 (2010). Section 1101 (a)(6) of the Dodd-Frank Act amended section 13(3) of the Federal Reserve Act restricting the authority of the Federal Reserve to make emergency loans to a particular institution. See Coffee (2012: 1059-1061), presenting opposing views as to whether this restriction effectively limits the power of the Federal Reserve to bail out distressed banks.

90 Dodd-Frank Act, Title II, creating an Orderly Liquidation Authority. But see Acharya & Öncü (2013: 300-309), emphasizing the limits of this solution in guaranteeing against the need to bail out Systemically Important Financial Institutions (so-called SIFIs).

Although the current crisis of the Eurozone is more complex, much can be learned from this analysis of the global financial crisis. In my future research in law and finance, I will try to sort out the consequences of uncertainty for the stability and growth of the European Union.

But I can already argue that, compared with the United States, the Eurozone suffers from the absence of centralized supervision and resolution of banks. To be sure, the E.U. Council is committed to establishing a European Banking Union as of 2014. Pursuant to article 127, paragraph 6, of the Treaty on the Functioning of the European Union, the European Central Bank is set to become the supervisor of the largest banks of the Eurozone.[91] However, this is not a *real* Banking Union because it still leaves bank resolution and deposit insurance in the hands of national authorities.[92] This is not good for incentives.[93] Because national authorities may be unwilling, or unable, to resolve a bankrupt bank, the European Central Bank will end up supporting zombie banks because of lack of viable alternatives.

In my opinion, it should not work this way. In the lending of last resort as I have advocated, central banks are disciplined because, if they fail to distinguish illiquidity from insolvency, they make losses. Central banks can credibly operate even with negative equity for two reasons: a) they are backed by governments; b) they can print money. On the one hand, this unique feature makes central banks a credible backstop against uncertainty. On the other hand, should central banks make losses and deal with them either way, their independence would be compromised. Particularly unbridled inflation would be the end of story for a central bank. The problem, in Europe, is that the failure

---

91 According to Art. 127(6) TFEU: 'The Council, acting by means of regulations in accordance with a special legislative procedure, may unanimously, and after consulting the European Parliament and the European Central Bank, confer specific tasks upon the European Central Bank concerning policies relating to the prudential supervision of credit institutions and other financial institutions with the exception of insurance undertakings.' A unanimous agreement to confer upon the European Central Bank the direct supervision of the largest banks of the Eurozone (along with the establishment of a Single Supervisory Mechanism, SSM, for all the banks) was reached in the ECOFIN Council on 13 December 2012. After negotiations with the European Commission and the European Parliament on the other instruments of legislation requiring their consent, an agreement was reached on 19 March 2013. The SSM is set to become effective 12 months after the entry into force of the legislation, which is not yet published at the time of writing. See 'Bank supervision: Council confirms agreement with EP', press release (with a link to the text agreed upon) available at www.consilium.europa.eu/uedocs/cms_data/docs/pressdata/en/ecofin/136846.pdf (last accessed on 12 June 2013).

92 Véron (2012).

93 See, in a similar vein, Schoenmaker (2012) and Wyplosz (2012a).

of one of the largest banks or sovereigns would likewise result in the death of the Eurozone. In order for central bankers to be on their toes in governing liquidity, they must have alternatives to self-destruction. Insolvency must not be their problem, but somebody else's.[94] Currently, this somebody else does not exist in the Eurozone.

At this point, I would like to indulge in my own science fiction. Assume that central banking around the world operate as I have advocated, perhaps even under some international agreement to that effect. Thus, central banks would provide a backstop to uncertainty, but they would still have the incentives to hold banks accountable for their losses. The question is, would that be enough to guarantee safe banking?

Hardly! Remember the rocket science bond, the innovation that we cannot predict? It will do wonders before the smartest central bankers realize that it's dangerous; then it will be too late. However, the good news is that central banks will have a precise mandate to backstop the illiquidity of that bond. The bad news on the other hand is that, counting on that backstop, private banks will take so much risk that they will become insolvent and creditors or taxpayers will have to foot the bill.

Corporate governance may help here, postponing the realization of profits and losses until the consequences of risk-taking are revealed.

This is the goal of the recent regulations of bankers' remuneration. In the U.S., the Dodd-Frank Act compels listed companies to claw back the incentive pay of executives in the presence of earnings restatements.[95] In the E.U., article 88 of the forthcoming Capital Requirements Directive sets rigorous limits on bankers' remuneration, which are partly relaxed if performance pay is deferred.[96] The problem for incentives, however, is not that bankers earn too much money, but that they may take their money and run before the bank goes bankrupt, and perhaps is bailed out.[97] To cope with such a situation, it makes sense to defer bankers' performance-based pay until well after the end of their term.[98] Bankers would think twice before taking too much risk, because their destiny would be tied to that of the banks they are dooming

---

94 Brunnermeier & Gersbach (2012) have an interesting proposal on how to fix this incentives problem.

95 Section 954 of the Dodd-Frank Act. However, at the time of writing, this is still one of the many provisions of the Dodd-Frank Act that awaits implementation by the Securities and Exchange Commission.

96 See Art. 88 of the CRD proposal.

97 Bebchuk & Spamann (2010).

98 Bhagat & Romano (2009).

to fail. Strangely, however, there is no clear evidence that all bankers took their money and ran during the global financial crisis.[99]

While the last observation confirms that moral hazard is not crucial in the presence of uncertainty, it is also evidence of another problem. If bank managers engage in moral hazard, they do it in the interest of shareholders, not against their interest.[100] Therefore, regulating bankers' pay isn't enough so long as the management is under the influence of shareholders. Although it is possible to make bankers accountable to other stakeholders, like creditors and governments, we still want banking to be driven by profit and be efficient. Hence shareholders should always play a role.

Short-termism undermines the efficiency of the shareholder franchise in banking. If shareholders can take the money and run too, it is not surprising that they set managers on a similar incentive scheme. Shareholders as a group can take cash out of a bank in two ways: dividends and takeovers.[101] As I mentioned, Basel 3 and its implementation will allow limiting dividend pay-out.[102] Takeovers should be restricted too. However, because takeovers also incentivize efficient management, they should not be prohibited, but coordinated with the regulation of managerial remuneration.

Managers facing a mandatory deferral of performance pay will ask that their salary be increased considerably to compensate the risk that shareholders fire them for temporary underperformance.[103] It would be cheaper for shareholders – and better for society – if managers were allowed to resist dismissal and enjoy private benefits of control. Private benefits of control commit shareholders to a long-term view. Takeovers could still replace inefficient bankers, but shareholders would need to compensate managers with a golden parachute before they could take any cash from the deal.[104]

Although the recent legislation seeks to defer bankers' performance pay, company law often prevents from fixing the other incentives in

---

99 Compare Bebchuk, Cohen, & Spamann (2010) with Fahlenbrach & Stulz (2011). See also Becht, Bolton, & Roell (2012) for a discussion of the empirical evidence.

100 Ferreira, Kershaw, Kirchmaier, & Schuster (2013) provide empirical evidence that, in the U.S., banks in which shareholders were more powerful performed worse during the global financial crisis. See also Beltratti & Stulz (2012) (banks with more shareholder-friendly corporate governance performed poorly in the global financial crisis).

101 See Mayer (2013), likewise arguing that private benefits of control commit shareholders to a long term view.

102 See *supra* text to notes 72-74.

103 Pacces (2013).

104 Pacces (2009).

the articles of association. In most E.U. jurisdictions, takeover defences and golden parachutes are restricted.[105] Lifting those restrictions would enable both managers and shareholders of banks to commit to long-term performance. And, with long-term market prices disciplining the allocation of finance, central banks could confidently take care that the system does not go off the rails because of uncertainty in the short term.

105 In Pacces (2012) I discuss this problem with specific reference to the U.K., the Netherlands, Sweden, and Italy. Enriques, Gilson, & Pacces (2013) present the general economic case for an 'unbiased' freedom of contract in takeover law.

6. Conclusion

I was told that the golden rules for a successful inaugural lecture are keeping it to 45 minutes and being able to summarize it in one sentence. So here is my summary.

In law and finance, the future is complicated by moral hazard and uncertainty: curbing moral hazard, the law supports market discipline; managing uncertainty, the law stops market discipline from crippling the world.

Let me conclude with some words of thanks. I am grateful to the Netherlands, the Erasmus University and the Erasmus School of Law for hosting me and giving me the opportunity to become a professor – something I always wanted to become. This could not have happened without Roger Van den Bergh. Not only did he infect me with the law and economics virus almost 20 years ago; he convinced me that I could infect many more generations of students and scholars if I moved to academia. I met Roger for the first time in the office of Roberto Pardolesi. Roberto had in fact already infected me. Whatever I have not learned directly from them, I discovered thanks to their advice.

I thank the University's Board for having offered me the prestigious Tinbergen tenure track that brought me here, and former Dean Marc Loth for nominating me for this post after obtaining my PhD. Those have been challenging years. I thank former Dean Maarten Kroeze for his encouragement; Michael Faure for his support and advice; and the other members of the Rotterdam Institute of Law and Economics, for being inspiring colleagues and good friends. I thank my students too: I learned from you more than just from reading dozens of papers.

I wish to thank the *Vereniging Trustfonds* of the Erasmus University for sponsoring my chair and giving me the opportunity to develop a law and finance scholarship here at the Erasmus School of Law. Special thanks go to the Dean, Suzan Stoter, and all the other professors of the School of Law for supporting this adventure, regardless of your own background, and honouring me with your presence here today.

After so many years in Rotterdam, the other colleagues, friends and neighbours to whom I am indebted are just too many to mention. But I want to thank especially the Italians who came to attend this lecture, and in particular the Ambassador of Italy whose presence is a great honour for me. Thanks also to Jon Klick, Colin Mayer and Neil Rickman who crossed some little and some big water to be here today.

In his regrets, Marc Loth wished me many more happy years in Rotterdam. After spending 45 minutes trying to persuade you that the future can't be predicted, all I can say is that I'd love that wish to come true. But Rotterdam has already granted me a lot of happiness, not only professionally as I said, but also personally. In Rotterdam I met my wife Olia; our son Leonardo was born in Rotterdam; and in Rotterdam we happily live together. I thank my family for their patience, support, and for filling my life with joy.

Finally, I thank my parents and my brother for coming here today and seeing this joy.

Grazie, mamma, papà ed Eriprando di essere qui.

Ik heb gezegd.

References

Acharya, V.V. & Öncü, T.S. 2013, 'A Proposal for the Resolution of Systemically Important Assets and Liabilities: The Case of the Repo Market', *International Journal of Central Banking*, vol. 9, no. S1, pp. 291-349.

Admati, A.R. & Hellwig, M. 2013, *The Bankers' New Clothes: What's Wrong With Banking and What to Do About it*, Princeton University Press.

Adrian, T. & Shin, H.S. 2010, 'Liquidity and Leverage', *Journal of Financial Intermediation*, vol. 19, no. 3, pp. 418-437.

Akerlof, G.A. & Shiller, R.J. 2009, *Animal Spirits: How Human Psychology Drives the Economy and Why it Matters for Global Capitalism*, Princeton University Press.

Bagehot, W. 1873, *Lombard Street: A Description of the Money Market*, Reprint 1915, John Murray, London.

Bebchuk, L.A. & Spamann, H. 2010, 'Regulating Bankers' Pay', *Georgetown Law Journal*, vol. 98, no. 2, pp. 247-287.

Bebchuk, L.A., Cohen, A. & Spamann, H. 2010, 'The Wages of Failure: Executive Compensation at Bear Stearns and Lehman 2000-2008', *Yale Journal of Regulation*, vol. 27, pp. 257-282.

Becht, M., Bolton, P. & Roell, A. 2012, 'Why Bank Governance is Different', *Oxford Review of Economic Policy*, vol. 27, no. 3, pp. 437-463.

Beltratti, A. & Stulz, R.M. 2012, 'The Credit Crisis Around the Globe: Why Did Some Banks Perform Better?', *Journal of Financial Economics*, vol. 105, no. 1, pp. 1-17.

Bernanke, B. 2012, *Some Reflections on the Crisis and the Policy Response*, Remarks delivered at the Russell Sage Foundation and Century Foundation Conference on 'Rethinking Finance', New York City (April 2012).

Bhagat, S. & Romano, R. 2009, 'Reforming Executive Compensation: Focusing and Committing to the Long-term', *Yale Journal on Regulation*, vol. 26, no. 2, pp. 359-372.

Brunnermeier, M.K. & Pedersen, L.H. 2009, 'Market Liquidity and Funding Liquidity', *Review of Financial Studies*, vol. 22, no. 6, pp. 2201-2238.

Brunnermeier, M.K. 2009, 'Deciphering the Liquidity and Credit Crunch 2007-2008', *Journal of Economic Perspectives*, vol. 23, no. 1, pp. 77-100.

Brunnermeier, M.K., Crockett, A., Goodhart, C., Persuad, A., & Shin, H. 2009. *The Fundamental Principles of Financial Regulation*, Geneva Reports on the World Economy No. 11, ICMB & CEPR, London.

Brunnermeier, M.K. & Gersbach, H. 2012, 'True Independence for the ECB: Triggering Power - No More, No Less', *Vox-EU* (20 December 2012), available at www.voxeu.org/article/true-independence-ecb-triggering-power-no-more-no-less (last accessed on 12 June 2013).

Caballero, R.J. & Krishnamurthy, A. 2008, 'Collective Risk Management in a Flight to Quality Episode', *Journal of Finance,* vol. 63, no. 5, pp. 2195-2230.

Caballero, R.J. & Kurlat, P.D. 2009, 'The 'Surprising' Origin and Nature of Financial Crises: a Macroeconomic Policy Proposal', MIT Department of Economics Working Paper No. 09-24 (September 2009). Available at SSRN: http://ssrn.com/abstract=1473918 (last accessed on 12 June 2012).

Caballero, R.J. & Krishnamurthy, A. 2011, 'Global Imbalances and Financial Fragility', *American Economic Review,* vol. 99, no. 2, pp. 584-588.

Caballero, R.J. & Farhi, E. 2013, 'A Model of the Safe Asset Mechanism (SAM): Safety Traps and Economic Policy', National Bureau of Economic Research, Working Paper No. 18737 (January 2013).

Calomiris, C.W. 2009, 'The Subprime Turmoil: What's Old, What's New, and What's Next', *Journal of Structured Finance,* vol. 15, no. 1, pp. 6-52.

Coase, R.H. 1960, 'The Problem of Social Cost', *Journal of Law and Economics,* vol. 3, pp. 1-44.

Coase, R.H. 1992, 'The Institutional Structure of Production', *American Economic Review,* vol. 82, no. 4, pp. 713-719.

Coffee, J.C. 2012, 'The Political Economy of Dodd-Frank: Why Financial Reform Tends to Be Frustrated and Systemic Risk Perpetuated', *Cornell Law Review,* vol. 97, pp. 1019-1082.

Cooter, R.D. & Ulen, T. 2011, *Law and Economics,* 6th edn, Pearson/ Addison Wesley, Boston, MA.

Dang, T.V., Gorton, G. & Holmström, B. 2012, 'Ignorance, Debt and Financial Crises', Working Paper, Yale University (February 2012).

De Grauwe, P. 2012, 'The Governance of a Fragile Eurozone', *Australian Economic Review,* vol. 45, no. 3, pp. 255-268.

Dewatripont, M., Rochet, J. & Tirole, J. 2010, *Balancing the Banks: Global Lessons from the Financial Crisis,* Princeton University Press.

Dewatripont, M. & Tirole, J. 2012, 'Macroeconomic Shocks and Banking Regulation' *Journal of Money, Credit and Banking,* vol. 44, pp. 237-254.

Diamond, D.W. & Dybvig, P.H. 1983, 'Bank Runs, Deposit Insurance, and Liquidity', *Journal of Political Economy,* vol. 91, no. 3, pp. 401-419.

Duffie, J.D. & Skeel, D. 2012, 'A Dialogue on the Costs and Benefits of Automatic Stays for Derivatives and Repurchase Agreements', University of Pennsylvania, Institute for Law & Economics Research Paper No. 12-02.

Enriques, L., Gilson, R.J. & Pacces, A.M. 2013, 'The Case for an Unbiased Takeover Law (with an Application to the European Union)', ECGI-Law Working Paper No. 212/2013 (May 2013). Available at SSRN: http://ssrn.com/abstract=2258926 (last accessed on 12 June 2012).

Fahlenbrach, R. & Stulz, R.M. 2011, 'Bank CEO Incentives and the Credit Crisis', *Journal of Financial Economics,* vol. 99, no. 1, pp. 11-26.

Ferreira, D., Kershaw, D., Kirchmaier, T. & Schuster, E. 2013, 'Shareholder Empowerment and Bank Bailouts', ECGI-Finance Working Paper No. 345/2013 (May 2013). Available at SSRN: http://ssrn.com/abstract=2170392 (last accessed on 12 June 2012).

Financial Stability Board 2011, 'Shadow Banking: Scoping the Issues' (April 2011), available at www.financialstabilityboard.org/publications/ r_110412a.pdf (last accessed on 12 June 2013).

Frydman, R. & Goldberg, M.D. 2011, *Beyond Mechanical Markets: Asset Price Swings, Risk, and the Role of the State,* Princeton University Press.

Geanakoplos, J. 2010, 'Solving the Present Crisis and Managing the Leverage Cycle', *Federal Reserve Bank of New York Economic Policy Review,* August 2010, pp. 101-113.

Gennaioli, N., Shleifer, A. & Vishny, R.W. 2013, 'A Model of Shadow Banking', *Journal of Finance* (vol. 68, no. 4, pp. 1331-1363).

Gorton, G.B. 2009, 'The Subprime Panic', *European Financial Management,* vol. 15, no. 1, pp. 10-46.

Gorton, G.B. 2010a, 'Questions and Answers about the Financial Crisis', National Bureau of Economic Research, Working Paper No. 1578 (February 2010).

Gorton, G.B. 2010b, *Slapped by the Invisible Hand: The Panic of 2007,* Oxford University Press.

Gorton, G.B. & Metrick, A. 2010a, 'Haircuts', *Federal Reserve Bank of St. Louis Review,* vol. 92, no. 6, pp. 507-519.

Gorton, G.B. & Metrick, A. 2010b, 'Regulating the Shadow Banking System', *Brookings Papers on Economic Activity,* vol. 41, no. 2 (Fall), pp. 261-312.

Gorton, G.B. & Metrick, A. 2012, 'Securitized Banking and the Run on Repo', *Journal of Financial Economics,* vol. 104, no. 3, pp. 425-451.

Gorton, G.B. & Ordoñez, G. 2012, 'Collateral crises', National Bureau of Economic Research, Working Paper No. 17771 (January 2012).

Gorton, G.B. 2012, 'Some Reflections on the Recent Financial Crisis', National Bureau of Economic Research, Working Paper No. 18397 (September 2012).

He, Z., Khang, I.G. & Krishnamurthy, A. 2010, 'Balance Sheet Adjustments During the 2008 Crisis', *IMF Economic Review,* vol. 58, no. 1, pp. 118-156.

Hegel, G. W. F. 1802, *Phenomenology of Spirit,* Preface, available at www.marxists.org/reference/archive/hegel/works/ph/phprefac.htm (last accessed on 12 June 2013).

Hellwig, M. 2008, 'The Causes of the Financial Crisis', *CESifo Forum,* vol. 9, no. 4, pp. 12-21.

Hellwig, M. 2009, 'Systemic Risk in the Financial Sector: An Analysis of the Subprime-Mortgage Financial Crisis', *De Economist,* vol. 157, no. 2, pp. 129-207.

Heremans, D. & Pacces, A.M. 2012, 'Regulation of Banking and Financial Markets' in R.J. Van den Bergh & A.M. Pacces (eds.), *Regulation and Economics,* Encyclopedia Law and Economics, 2nd edn., Edward Elgar, Cheltenham, pp. 558-606.

International Monetary Fund 2008, *Global Financial Stability Report – Financial Stress and Deleveraging: Macro-Financial Implications and Policy* (October 2008), IMF, Washington, DC.

International Monetary Fund 2010, *Global Financial Stability Report – Sovereigns, Funding, and Systemic Liquidity* (October 2010), IMF, Washington, DC.

Johnson, S. & Kwak, J. 2010, *13 Bankers: The Wall Street Takeover and the Next Financial Meltdown,* Pantheon Books, New York.

Keynes, J.M. 1921, *A Treatise on Probability.* Reprint 1973 (The Collected Writings of John Maynard Keynes, Vol. VIII), Macmillan, London.

Keynes, J.M. 1936, *The General Theory of Employment, Interest and Money,* Reprint 2008, BN Publishing, Milton Keynes.

Keynes, J.M. 1937, 'The General Theory of Employment', *Quarterly Journal of Economics,* vol. 51, no. 2, pp. 209-223.

Klick, J. 2013, 'Shleifer's Failure', *Texas Law Review,* vol. 91, pp. 899-961.

Knight, F.H. 1921, *Risk, Uncertainty and Profit,* Houghton Mifflin, Boston, MA.

Krishnamurthy, A. 2010, 'Amplification Mechanisms in Liquidity Crises', *American Economic Journal: Macroeconomics,* vol. 2, no. 3, pp. 1-30.

La Porta, R., Lopez-de-Silanes, F., Shleifer, A. & Vishny, R.W. 1998, 'Law and Finance', *Journal of Political Economy,* vol. 106, no. 6, pp. 1113-1155.

La Porta, R., Lopez-de-Silanes, F. & Shleifer, A. 2008, 'The Economic Consequences of Legal Origins', *Journal of Economic Literature,* vol. 46, no. 2, pp. 285-332.

Levine, R. 1999, 'Law, Finance, and Economic Growth', *Journal of Financial Intermediation,* vol. 8, no. 1-2, pp. 8-35.

Levine, R. 2005, 'Finance and Growth: Theory and Evidence' in P. Aghion & S. Durlauf, *Handbook of Economic Growth,* Elsevier, Amsterdam, pp. 865-934.

Levine, R. 2011, *Regulating Finance and Regulators to Promote Growth.* Working Paper (August 2011). Available at http://faculty.haas.berkeley.edu/ross_levine/papers.htm (last accessed on 12 June 2013).

Mayer, C. 2013, *Firm Commitment: Why the Corporation is Failing Us and How to Restore Trust in it,* Oxford University Press.

Mehrling, P. 2011, *The New Lombard Street: How the Fed Became the Dealer of Last Resort,* Princeton University Press.

Minsky, H.P. 1975, *John Maynard Keynes,* Reprint 2008, McGraw-Hill, New York.

Minsky, H.P. 1986, *Stabilizing an Unstable Economy,* Reprint 2008, McGraw-Hill, New York.

Organization for Economic Co-operation and Development 2012, *Economic Outlook No. 92* (December 2012), OECD, Paris.

Pacces, A.M. 2009, 'Control Matters: Law and Economics of Private Benefits of Control', ECGI-Law Working Paper No. 131/2009 (August 2009). Available at SSRN: http://ssrn.com/abstract=1448164 (last accessed on 12 June 2012).

Pacces, A.M. 2010, 'Consequences of Uncertainty for Regulation: Law and Economics of the Financial Crisis', *European Company and Financial Law Review,* vol. 7, no. 4, pp. 479-511.

Pacces, A.M. 2011, 'How does Corporate Law Matter? Law and Finance and Beyond', in M. Faure & J. Smits (eds.), *Does Law Matter? On Law and Economic Growth,* Intersentia, Antwerp, pp. 297-329.

Pacces, A.M. 2012, *Rethinking Corporate Governance: The Law and Economics of Control Powers,* Routledge, Abingdon.

Pacces, A.M. 2013, 'Illiquidity and Financial Crisis', *University of Pittsburgh Law Review,* vol. 74, no. 3 (forthcoming).

Park, S. 2011, 'The Size of the Subprime Shock', Korea Advanced Institute of Science and Technology, Working Paper (on file with author).

Perotti, E. & Suarez, J. 2009, 'Liquidity Insurance for Systemic Crises', CEPR Policy Insight No. 31 (February 2009).

Perotti, E. 2010, 'Systemic Liquidity Risk and Bankruptcy Exceptions', CEPR Policy Insight No. 8 (October 2010).

Pistor, K. 2012, 'Towards a Legal Theory of Finance', CEPR Discussion Paper No. 9235 (November 2012).

Posner, R.A. 2009, *A Failure of Capitalism: The Crisis of '08 and the Descent into Depression,* Harvard University Press, Cambridge, MA.

Posner, R.A. 2010, 'On the Receipt of the Ronald H. Coase Medal: Uncertainty, the Economic Crisis, and the Future of Law and Economics', *American Law and Economics Review,* vol. 12, no. 2, pp. 280-318.

Rajan, R.G. & Zingales, L. 1998, 'Financial Dependence and Growth', *American Economic Review,* vol. 113, no. 2, pp. 559-586.

Reichlin, L., Turner, A. & Woodford, M. 2013 'Helicopter Money as a Policy Option', *Vox-EU* (20 May 2013), available at www.voxeu.org/article/helicopter-money-policy-option (last accessed on 12 June 2013).

Reinhart, C.M. & Rogoff, K.S. 2009, 'The Aftermath of Financial Crises', *American Economic Review,* vol. 99, no. 2, pp. 466-472.

Roncaglia, A. 2012, 'Keynesian Uncertainty and the Shaky Foundations of Statistical Risk Assessment Models', *PSL Quarterly Review,* vol. 65, no. 263, pp. 335-383.

Roubini, N. & Mihm, S. 2010, *Crisis Economics – A Crash Course in the Future of Finance,* Penguin Press, New York.

Runde, J. 1994, 'Keynesian Uncertainty and Liquidity Preference', *Cambridge Journal of Economics,* vol. 18, no. 2, pp. 129-144.

Schoenmaker, D. 2012 'Banking Union: Where We're Going Wrong' in T. Beck (ed.) *Banking Union for Europe,* CEPR & Vox-EU, London, pp. 97-103.

Shiller, R.J. 2008, *The Subprime Solution: How Today's Global Financial Crisis Happened, and What to Do About it,* Princeton University Press.

Shleifer, A. & Vishny, R. 2011, 'Fire Sales in Finance and Macroeconomics', *Journal of Economic Perspectives,* vol. 25, no. 1, pp. 29-48.

Thaler, R.H. & Sunstein, C.R. 2003, 'Libertarian Paternalism', *American Economic Review,* vol. 93, no. 2, pp. 175-179.

Tirole, J. 2006, *The Theory of Corporate Finance,* Princeton University Press.

Véron, N. 2012, 'Europe Takes an Important Step Towards a European Banking Union', *Vox-EU* (19 December 2012), available at www.voxeu.org/article/europe-takes-important-step-towards-european-banking-union (last accessed on 12 June 2013).

Wyplosz, C. 2012a, 'Banking Union as a Crisis-Management Tool' in T. Beck (ed.) *Banking Union for Europe,* CEPR & Vox-EU, London, pp. 19-23.

Wyplosz, C. 2012b, 'Thanks to the ECB', *Vox-EU* (30 July 2012), available at http://www.voxeu.org/article/thanks-ecb (last accessed on 12 June 2013).

Zingales, L. 2010, 'Learning to Live with Not-So-Efficient Markets', *Daedalus,* vol. 139, no. 4, pp. 31-40.

Inaugural lecture of Alessio M. Pacces at Erasmus School of Law

'The future in law and finance'

26 April 2013

Abstract

The success of a capitalist economy rests upon the ability of finance to sustain potentially infinite growth, based on funding today the output of tomorrow. Finance, however, needs rules. The aim of the law and finance scholarship is precisely to identify the best regulation of finance to support economic growth.

Traditionally, law and finance is concerned with investor protection. This would be sufficient if the future was predictable. However, because the future is in fact uncertain, the prices of financial assets are flawed and in the short run they may result in serious mistakes, if not widespread crises. Although these mistakes are corrected in the long run, a lot of harm may occur in the meantime.

Financial law should therefore be concerned not only with investor protection, but also with mitigating the temporary excesses of markets in allowing or restricting access to finance. The challenge of this goal is to remedy market myopia without allowing policymakers to abuse the power of governments. However imperfect, prices remain the best instrument of discipline and growth in a market economy.

Inaugurele rede van Alessio M. Pacces aan de Faculteit der Rechtsgeleerdheid van de Erasmus Universiteit

'The future in law and finance'

26 april 2013

Samenvatting

Het succes van de kapitalistische economieën is gebaseerd op de mogelijkheid van financiering om de productie van morgen kracht bij te zetten door de financiële middelen van vandaag. In potentie gaat het hierbij om oneindige groei. Financiering heeft echter regelgeving nodig. Het doel van *law and finance* onderzoek is gelegen in het vinden van de beste regulering van financiering die de economische groei ondersteunt.

Law and finance is van oudsher gericht op de bescherming van financiers. Dat zou genoeg zijn als de toekomst voorspelbaar was. Omdat de toekomst in werkelijkheid onzeker is, vertonen de prijzen van financiële activa gebreken en kunnen op de korte termijn tot grote vergissingen of zelfs een wereldwijde crisis leiden. Ondanks dat deze vergissingen op de lange termijn hersteld worden, kan in de tussentijd veel schade ontstaan.

Het financieel recht moet daarom niet alleen gericht zijn op de bescherming van financiers, maar ook op het inperken van de excessen van de markten bij het toestaan of beperken van de toegang tot financiering. De uitdaging van dit doel is het herstellen van de blinde vlekken in de marktwerking, zonder toe te staan dat beleidsmakers misbruik kunnen maken van de macht van overheden. Uiteindelijk blijven marktprijzen, hoe gebrekkig die ook kunnen zijn, het beste instrument voor regeling en groei van de markteconomie.

Lectio Inauguralis di Alessio M. Pacces presso l'università Erasmus di Rotterdam

'THE FUTURE IN LAW AND FINANCE'

26 Aprile 2013

Riassunto

Il successo di una economia capitalistica dipende dalla capacità della finanza di sostenere una crescita potenzialmente infinita, finanziando oggi la produzione di domani. La finanza, però, ha bisogno di regole. *Law and finance* è appunto la disciplina che ambisce a individuare il miglior diritto finanziario per la crescita.

Tradizionalmente *law and finance* significa protezione degli investitori. Questo basterebbe se il futuro fosse prevedibile. Siccome in realtà il futuro è incerto e imprevedibile, i prezzi che si formano sui mercati finanziari sono imperfetti e possono dar luogo a gravi errori, se non vere e proprie crisi, nel breve periodo. Anche se questi errori vengono corretti nel lungo periodo, i danni intermedi sono spesso irreparabili.

Il diritto della finanza si deve allora occupare non solo della protezione degli investitori, ma anche di mitigare gli eccessi temporanei dei mercati nel regolare l'accesso alla finanza. La sfida di questo obiettivo è rimediare alla miopia dei mercati senza consentire ai regolatori di abusare dei loro poteri normativi. I prezzi, per quanto imperfetti, restano il miglior strumento di disciplina e di crescita di una economia di mercato.